Risk It!

How to Run
Great Events and
Live with the Risk

Paul Cook

Richard John

Risk It!
How to Run Great Events and Live with the Risk

First published in Great Britain by Planet Planit Ltd

www.planetplanit.biz

Designed and typeset by Design Inspiration
designinspiration.co.uk

A CIP catalogue record for this book is available from the British Library.

Contents

Introduction

Thanks for picking up this book. Just to be clear, this is a book addressing the issues of event risk planning and insurance, which are probably not the most exciting topics you've ever considered.

But we are really keen to get the message across that NOTHING ever happens without some degree of risk, and we want you to continue to stretch yourself by creating the most exciting and innovative events possible.

Everything we do in life has some element of risk; whether that is crossing the road, asking someone for a date, producing a new product or creating your most successful event ever.

In fact we believe that, without risk there would be no progress.

So why in the events world do we attempt to run events without risk? It can never happen; in life, there is always a risk of some description. So, rather than running away we want you to embrace risk because then you can really move forward and create your own success.

We think that risk planning is an important and neglected issue. And every day the newspapers, magazines and World Wide Web are full of stories which support our view.

But we're guessing that you didn't go into the world of events because of the opportunity to spend your time completing risk assessment forms, and getting scared at the stories of what could go wrong. The truth is, neither did we.

That's why we've written this book from the point of view of event practitioners, avoiding lots of tedious jargon, and making this as much of a "how to" and a "how not to" guide as possible.

Our intention is to make you aware of the things that can go wrong (and actually have gone wrong) so that you don't make the same mistakes (it's generally OK if you make new ones!)

If the book raises some questions that it doesn't answer, well, that is ok as well as the issue of risk is always present and there will always be new risks to deal with.

We would love to take your questions, comments and feedback and you will find our contact details in the back of the book.

But if you've made the commitment to buy and read this book, then good on you. It shows you're serious about making events as safe and successful as possible. We wish you every success.

We'd like to say a big "thank you" for buying it and proving there was a real need for it, and give an even bigger "thanks" to the supporters who made this book a reality. You know who you are. And we salute you.

Paul Cook   *Richard John*

How to Use This Book

This is how we'd like to suggest you use this book: Take a few minutes to familiarise yourself with the layout and contents. You'll see it's all very straightforward.

Then consider who you'd like to share it with. After all, there's no reason why you should have to carry everything on your own shoulders.

You will see we address the issues of what might go wrong; it's not our intention to worry you unduly; the likelihood is you'll never have any issue at any of your events. But just in case...

There's a wealth of generic content that tells you how to address the virtuous circle: that's "plan/do/act/review." (And, whilst we have used the planning of an event as our model you can apply the same ideas/methods for any number of different businesses.)

When you are working on your next event, you might find it useful to use and share the planning process so that risk planning can be sorted out, allowing you to get on with the fun (!) elements of your event.

This book can be read in one sitting, but it should also serve as a guide to dip into whenever you have an event to think about.

To help with this we have divided the book into four main sections; Events and Risks, Your Toolkit for Peace of Mind, Insurance and Sector Challenges.

Within each section there are separate chapters.

You'll notice we've kept the language and the examples as simple as possible.

We felt this was particularly important with the Insurance section.

However, as with most industries a few words and phrases have crept in that may be a little confusing and mysterious to those on the outside, so you'll find a Simple and Short Glossary of (mainly) Insurance Terms that may make things simpler.

Our choice has been to use the term 'event planner' but we know that event organiser, meeting planner etc could also have been used.

In the same way 'insurance company' could also be substituted for insurance syndicate or underwriting agency.

Finally, we take a quick look at the future risks and finish by including those all important references for the major events that we refer to in the text.

Section 1:
Events & Risks

Risk It

Section 1: Events & Risks

What Could Possibly Go Wrong With a Simple Event?

For many individuals and organisations involved with the events industry, the idea of worrying about something going wrong would seem to be an unnecessary pastime. After all, how dangerous can it be?

For example, you have to organise a simple meeting. So you phone a hotel, make a booking, people turn up, some presentations are made, lots of food is eaten and everyone goes home happy. Right?

The answer is yes and no. You see, the world of events has grown rapidly; a huge industry and academia has built up around the subject, and it is a major employer.

Events – Definition
In fact, it's worth defining an "event"; the emerit International Competency Standards' definition is: "a gathering of any size; that is held at a particular time; at a particular place; for a particular purpose; one time or recurring; publicly or privately; in an urban or rural setting; indoors or outdoors; at one or more locations."

Events – Types
So under the banner of 'events' we could be talking about:

Workshops
These are usually smaller events, usually run for educational or training purposes. They are often the type of training events undertaken in a hotel or similar venue.

Meetings, Seminars and Lectures
These are normally larger events; e.g. a workshop suggests delegate involvement, so numbers might be limited to 12; whereas a lecture implies more of a presentation from one or more "experts", and the audience might number in excess of 200.

Conferences, Conventions and Congresses
These are various kinds of larger events, and the names are interchangeable; for example, it's more usual to hear the term "convention" in the US and "congress' in Europe. They usually involve hundreds or even thousands of delegates descending on a region, and can have a major economic, social and political impact.

Celebratory Events
Celebratory events such as award ceremonies usually involve a sit-down dinner followed by various groups heading on stage to receive a trophy.

Product Launches
Where customers and prospects are brought to a venue to be exposed to the latest line of new products, usually launched with some theatrical flourish.

Press Launches
Where the audience are members of the Press, sometimes receiving a briefing in a traditional venue and on occasion taken to an exotic and expensive location in the hope that the press will write something positive.

Exhibitions
Where an organisation builds a stand at a trade or public exhibition (sometimes referred to as a fair).

Incentives
Winners of various company competitions are taken to possibly an exotic location as a reward, and encouraged to do even better next time.

Sporting Events
Events that are based around sport, which can be primarily concerned with corporate hospitality.

Field Marketing Events

This is a growing sector of the events market. Here, companies can be found handing out samples of products in shopping centres or railway stations (anywhere, in fact, where there's a decent number of relevant target consumers).

Additionally, some companies use the "stunt marketing" approach (sometimes known as "guerrilla events") to raise awareness and secure the all-important press coverage. Sir Richard Branson of The Virgin Group of Companies is an excellent example, often launching new Virgin businesses by abseiling down buildings and ballooning around the world.

Team-Building Activities

These are becoming increasingly popular. These may include undertaking sporting activities, or challenges such as film-making. Many companies will now wish to incorporate something socially beneficial, such as painting a school, or cleaning a park for the local community.

Legal Events

Public companies have a legal obligation (in the UK) to hold an Annual General Meeting (AGM) to which anyone who owns a share is entitled to attend.

Music Festivals and Concerts

Events focused around music and entertainment.

Commercial Events

Organising events as part of a business, whether as an agency, a commercial conference organiser, or a body such as a trade association. Such events form the backbone of the meetings industry and are hugely valuable to the economy.

Outdoor Events

These could include agricultural shows, car boot sales, religious gatherings or corporate parties to name but a few.

Multi – Category Events

Events that straddle a number of the previous categories, e.g. a conference with team-building activities, some of which are run outdoors.

It's important to understand just how vast the "events" sector has become and appreciate how your next meeting could take in several of these areas.

For example, your annual company event might include the traditional "meeting" element, listening to presentations, but will probably also include some activities, team-building and maybe a dinner and dance in the evening. Each of which will involve a different set of risks.

The Event Risk Triangle

Regardless of the events you will be involved with, we recommend that you consider what would be a "risk" for you, your organisation, stakeholder or clients. These could include (obvious examples such as):

Financial loss
Damage to property (yours, or someone else's)
Damage to reputation (corporate and individual)
Injury or death

There are far more risks than we would like but effectively they break down into two main types; Natural/Climatic and Man-Made. That is all there is.

We have created our simple 'event risk triangle' (Figure 1).

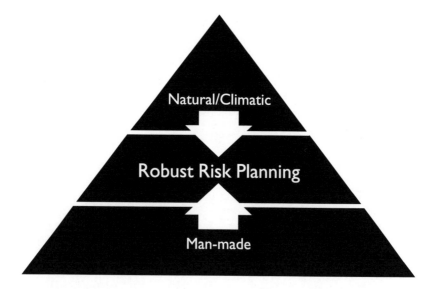

Figure 1 — The Event Risk Triangle

This shows the relationship of risks and the impact that they can have on your event and hence your need for a robust risk plan.

Developing your risk plan is investigated in Section 2 – Your Toolkit for Peace of Mind.

Quite purposely we have used a triangle which is a dynamic shape to illustrate the changing and moving nature of risks.

Here are just some examples of the risks that occur.

Natural/Climatic	Man Made
Snow	Financial stability
Ice	Political changes
Typhoon	Legislative changes
Wind	Terrorism
Storm	Theft
Flood	Food poisoning
Earthquake	Injury to people
Volcanic ash cloud	Brand reputation

There are of course many more but the good news is that not all of these will affect your event.

Event Risks – What's Out There?

If you've looked at our brief selection of risks, you may have started to consider all those things which could go wrong with your next event.

Those risks also exist in the run-up to your event, as well as on the day itself, and you should start considering the risks from the moment your event is conceived.

Successful events, where risk is minimised, are those where the process of handling risk is built-in right from the start, not bolted on at the last minute.

To make it easier for you to address risk issues, we've listed them under various headings, with some examples from real-life events.

Natural/Climatic Risks

The last few years have seen a number of high-profile natural disasters which have had a major impact, and not just on events.

When disaster strikes the ramifications can be far-reaching.

For example, in January 2010 the earthquake in Haiti led to a major international relief operation. The country is still struggling to recover.

For event planners, a bigger impact was caused by the eruption of an Icelandic volcano (Eyjafjallajokull) which erupted in April 2010, sending vast quantities of ash into the atmosphere.

Because of fears that this ash could clog the jet engines of aircraft, flights across Europe were completely suspended for several days, and then were only gradually reintroduced with major disruption to schedules.

Other forms of transport could accommodate only some of the disrupted passengers and at a far slower rate. Many planners had to accept smaller or cancelled events as a consequence.

As the dust settled from the volcano, May 2010 saw severe flooding in Tennessee, USA as a result of torrential rains.

Twenty one people died there and others in neighbouring states as a result. Numerous events were cancelled, deferred, or substantially reduced.

As a planner you have to be prepared to address all kinds of weather-related issues. Many of which will be unexpected.

So, whilst there may not be much you can do about Natural/Climatic risks, it's essential to be aware of what might happen.

Man Made Risks

For ease we have taken this vast category of risks and allocated certain incidents into types. But, however you look at this category the incidents are all due to man and not the force of nature.

Human Error

An analysis of event disasters would probably see most situations where things have gone wrong, on a small or large scale, as being due to "human error", a phrase which covers a multitude of sins.

You may like to think about your past events and whether "human error" has ever manifested itself. There may have been tiny issues, but did they have potential to be much worse?

For example, has anyone ever tripped over a power cable? Slipped on spilt liquid? Fallen over on stage? Has a presenter ever failed to turn up? Has the AV equipment ever malfunctioned and let you or one of your presenters down?

The examples just given tend to be among the most common insurance claims that are made. All those things could be listed as "human error", and many of them could have been avoided.

In 2006 at Katowice in Poland 65 people were killed when a roof collapsed at an exhibition centre. The snowfall had been unusually heavy, but charges were brought against the architects and building owners on the grounds that building specifications had not been met correctly.

During the music festival season of the 2010 Love Parade in Duisburg, 21 people were killed, and more than 500 injured near an overcrowded tunnel leading into the festival.

Safety experts and a fire service investigator had previously warned that the site was not suitable for the numbers expected to attend, and one consequence was that the planner announced the event festival , which had run since 1989, would never take place again.

And how often have we seen tragic pictures of the aftermath of fires in nightclubs; unfortunately, there have been far too many of those. Often the incidents are made worse because standard safety features, such as fire exits, have been locked or blocked, condemning people to death.

A simple internet search of the term "nightclub fire" will bring up pages of entries of accidents and injuries.

In all those examples, while there might have been other factors at play, it's safe to assume that the major issue that led to these incidents happening was simply "human error."

Accidents and Injuries

The likelihood is that your event won't go wrong; after all, on a daily basis, thousands of meetings, conferences, exhibitions, team-building sessions and other face to face marketing activities happen without anyone getting hurt.

But people do drink too much (on occasion) and it's not unknown for people to trip up at events, possibly due to a combination of alcohol, high heels (ladies), stress and bright lights.

It's also worth noting that the standards of safety vary tremendously around the world. Features such as grab handles and slip mats that you might take for granted in your own country won't necessarily be standard fittings when you run an event overseas.

Insurance claims are dominated by trips and slips, the simple incidents that can lead to a world of pain.

Terrorism

On September 11 2001 there were a number of conferences taking place in both the North and South towers of the World Trade Centre in New York, when they were struck by one of the world's most infamous terrorist attacks.

Terrorists have also struck in capital cities in Spain, the UK, France, Africa, India and Australasia in recent years. In fact, few parts of the world have not witnessed the indiscriminate acts of terrorism.

Sometimes, as shown by the IRA in London in the 1970s and 1980s, killing people was rarely part of their strategy; it was the economic disruption that perpetrators were looking to cause.

But sometimes bombers choose to strike without warning, with high civilian casualties being a central tenet of their objectives.

Companies with international brands, or strong associations with certain countries may be more liable for targeting, but the face of present-day terrorism suggests anyone can be a target.

Could this affect you or your clients? Well, there are plenty of people with a (often justified) concern about issues such as capitalism, the environment, animal rights, worker exploitation and a host of others.

However, while some choose to protest through letters and via the ballot box, a small minority will resort to violence to get their point made.

In the UK, for example, protesters targeting Huntingdon Life Science, the country's biggest vivisectionist, also attacked property, premises and people from any company providing services to HLS, no matter how tangential the link.

Some venues that hosted HLS meetings were among organisations that suffered until the authorities finally caught the perpetrators.

Theft

Major events can see huge amounts of dollars-worth of equipment being transported and set up, and each step of the journey can create the risk of valuable components being lost to theft.

At the other end of the scale, imagine how the overall success of your event could be tarred by a delegate having a wallet or phone stolen from a meeting room.

Simple steps to prevent these situations arising are all that's needed.

Reputation

A damaged reputation can cause much more than embarrassment; consider the financial loss caused to BP in 2010 by the explosion of an oil rig in the Gulf which cost lives and led to one of the US' worst environmental disasters.

Legislation

As a planner you may also need to make sure you don't fall foul of the increasing amount of legislation governing events.

For example, in many parts of the world, if you are organising an event, the doors won't be allowed to open until the relevant Authorities/Inspectors are satisfied, which means the more robust your planning and preparation, the easier their job will be.

You also need to ensure that you don't end up facing legal action because you have discriminated against particular groups. For example, the UK has the Disability Discrimination Act 1995 (DDA) which is rigorously enforced.

Event professionals in the USA will also be aware of the need to comply with the legal requirements of the Americans with Disabilities Act of 1990 for Disability provision requirements.

Corporate Espionage

It's worth remembering that not every country has the same attitude towards Intellectual Property (IP) and the value of Trade Marks and Copyright.

At some international trade shows it is common to see groups of people photographing all the new products on the opening morning and within hours there could be copies being made in some corner of the globe.

More recently, another type of espionage has appeared, known as "ambush marketing".

A recent famous example was seen at the 2010 World Cup in South Africa, involving Bavaria Beer (confusingly, a Dutch brand) and 36 women in orange mini skirts who went to the Netherlands vs Denmark football match.

The young women in mini dresses swayed appealingly for the camera with the aim of getting their brand noticed.

The girls were arrested, because "ambush marketing" is a criminal activity in South Africa. However, Bavaria Beer enjoyed much media coverage to the annoyance of the beer brand that had paid to be the "official" drink of the tournament.

So if you work for, or with, high profile brands, you may need to start thinking about developing an "anti-ambush marketing" strategy for your own events.

Political Activists

As we are seeing, "risks" can mean different things to different organisations. For example, a group of Canadian activists known as the 'Yes Men' sabotage events by pretending to be speakers from genuine organisations and then delivering, in a very professional and polished manner, a speech in which the most outrageous comments are made.

Often the delegates don't get the "joke", and many organisations and broadcasters have been fooled into broadcasting interviews from the Yes Men believing they are representatives of genuine companies.

The "Yes Men" have made two successful documentaries about their antics, so their identity is no secret; but if you were expecting guest speakers from a certain organisation, and some smartly-dressed men and women turn up as expected, how would you know they weren't the real thing?

Misbehaving

One of the biggest problems for event planners is that delegates can do stupid or thoughtless things, sometimes fuelled by alcohol or through peer pressure.

So dealing with the after-effects of such people and having plans in place to do so, can be a vital part of the role.

Don't be surprised to hear about delegates who are victims of minor crimes (such as theft) or scams that take place in unfamiliar cities.

Culture

Event planners will often be well-travelled people, but their delegates may be less so. So one of the risks to be managed may centre around different cultures, ethics and laws.

Or what about "service?" Giving gratuities is a commonly accepted practice in many parts of the world, and may be used to make basic salaries up to a decent level.

But when does "service" become "bribery?" When does a "token of thanks" become an attempt at corruption? Many companies are signatories to the 1997 OECD Anti-Bribery Convention.

The trouble is, as many event planners will testify, the difference between what seems logical and ethical when you are at your desk, and imperative when you are in a foreign land trying to get an event to come together.

Section 2:
Your Toolkit for Peace of Mind

Risk It

Risk It! How to Run Great Events and Live with the Risk

Section 2: Your Toolkit for Peace of Mind

We hope that you've had the chance to think about all the factors that could affect your events; in this section we're going to be looking at strategies for dealing with anything life might throw at you.

(a) Pre-Emptive Thinking

It's all in your Mind

You can picture your event; you know its objectives, and you know why you are putting it on. Quite simply, you are perfectly placed to know what could go wrong.

Does it really Matter?

We've looked at some of the many issues that could affect your event, and it's important that you understand what it could mean to you as the event planner. There are a number of issues but some of the key ones include:

- Your inability to pay staff or contractors for their services or products
- Your profit and loss account suffers
- You could go out of business.
- Your professional reputation is affected in a bad way.
- There could be damage to your kit or to the venue or location (this might prevent you from continuing in business)

However the good news is that if all your event elements are fully evaluated then the risks that can affect your event can be dealt with.

However, it is important to understand that there is no such thing as a "risk-free" event. That's because nothing in life is risk-free.

There is risk in everything we do every day of our lives and these include the simple things such as crossing the road or deciding to accept a new job.

When it comes to your event there will always be risk but the real professional planners will know how to make informed decisions to lessen the risk and the consequences to their event.

A 3 Way Split

An event has three key components; people, kit and money.

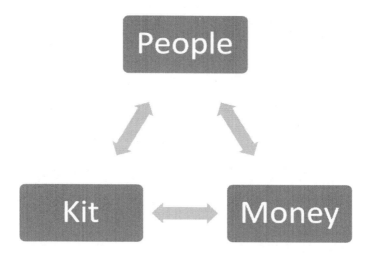

Figure 2 — Event Key Components

People

With no people you have no event. This is the case even if your event is "virtual" (i.e. based on the web).

Kit

For simplicity, our definition of 'kit' includes the venue or location. After all, you need a space for all those people that are coming to your event. Even if it is a virtual event you will need the proper equipment to make sure that all the communications work properly.

As well as the venue, our definition (in the People, Kit and Money concept) also includes all the portable equipment you will need to make your event work.

Money

Finally our third dynamic element is the one we all love, money. You may have the people, and you may have the kit (including venue) but without some money then you will not get very far.

Every event has an element of costs to be considered. Nothing is free. Even if your event has a number of contra deals attached to it (sometimes known as "barter", where no actual money changes hands) there will still be items that have to be paid for.

And, at the end of the day, you need to generate money to pay for your services and for you to stay in business.

So, having identified the 3 key components, let's look at them in more detail.

People

A diversity of people come together to produce events. Below are just some of the people that you will need (usually) to help you;

- Venue staff
- Artists and performers
- Speakers
- Delegates and participants
- General public
- Trade-only attendees
- Volunteers, stewards and helpers
- Your own staff
- Staff of other organisations
- Exhibitors
- Your Sub-Contractors
- Sub-Contractors of other parties
- Specialists/advisors of all types
- Police, Fire, Ambulance crews
- Press and media representatives

This is just a sample of the people you could be dealing with to make your event a success.

Sometimes you will need just a small number of these types of people (e.g. some events will not include exhibitors) but we hope this illustrates the scale of different categories of people.

What are they all bringing to the table?

Each person or organisation (known as a "party" in insurance jargon) should only be responsible for the part/role that they are actually playing in your event.

You will be required to insure some of the parties (by the law of the country) and for others you need to know that they have the necessary insurances in place. In those circumstances you need to do a quick check of their insurance, although it's essential to know what you're looking for.

This is especially important when dealing with contractors; if they cause an error that leads to a problem for you, who will be responsible for their negligence?

This is one of the reasons for you to know that they have some insurance in place that will deal with any damage/injury/financial loss that they cause.

(If you do not know what to ask for in insurance documentation then just ask your own insurance company/advisor or broker who will be able to help.)

But, to provide you with some ideas on how to get started here is our simple three step process.

Contractors Insurance Evidence – 3 Simple Steps

1. Ask for evidence of the Insurance

Dear ....

In accordance with our contract please can you arrange to supply to us a copy of your current ...... insurance policy and also confirm that the payment for the policy has been made to the insurance company.

2. When you receive the Insurance

You will be looking for:

Name of the Insurance company (ies)

Date(s) that the insurance policy is operative

Limit of Liability or Sum Insured

If in any doubt you should refer to your insurance broker/advisor/ company

3. Create a Spreadsheet of Insurance Evidence

Keep a simple spreadsheet of your contractors to keep up to date.

This will serve two main purposes:

It will remind you when to ask your contractor for details of their new insurance policy (as you will be keeping an eye on the expiry date)

It will be very useful for your insurance company should they ask you to prove the fact that you asked contractors for evidence of their insurance coverage (this is becoming increasingly common across all Liability insurers)

Figure 3 – Format for a Spreadsheet of Insurance Evidence

Contractor	Type of Insurance	Insurance Company	Policy Number	Expiry Date
Company A				
Company B				

In addition to holding evidence of the insurance for your contractor, make sure you know precisely what you need them to do for you.

Again a written agreement will make your life a lot simpler in the long run. It's also amazing how quickly people forget what they were supposed to be doing especially when facing a loss (as something has gone wrong).

Own Staff, Stewards and Volunteers
You also need to think about your own staff (including people such as stewards and volunteers) and how to ensure they are working in conditions that will not cause harm/injury to them?

In some countries there will be legal obligations that have to be met relating to the welfare of staff. Be sure to know what they are and how they can impact you even if you are not paying your volunteers or helpers.

Everyone Else
You should put yourself in the place of your delegates/public and work through what you are asking them to do whilst at your event. Is there anything dangerous that you need them to undertake? If there is, have a think about how you can make everything as safe as possible.

As a planner you may also have to consider how you will look after the people you will probably never meet.

For example, festival organisers have to think about keeping attendees and the general public safe from harm. Large events can attract amateur and professional criminals who know how vulnerable event-goers can be.

When it comes to dealing with large crowds control do you have enough security in place to make sure that there are no 'panics' should an unforeseen incident take place?

Regardless of the size of your next event, make sure, you have walked through the evacuation plan with the venue or location so that you know precisely what has to happen in the event of a crisis or emergency?

Many event planners believe that the chosen venue will automatically have insurance cover that they can rely on. There may be some venues that do this but the vast majority will expect you to have organised your own insurance.

They may not permit you to hold your event unless you can prove that you have the necessary "people cover". In industry jargon, that's known as Public (Third Party, General Commercial) Liability insurance.

You may also like to make sure that you have a copy of your company insurance, either as a hard copy, or as an electronic copy on your phone or laptop.

Although you may never have been asked, strictly speaking you should always be prepared to have a copy to show a venue.

Some very switched-on planners also have copies of important documentation such as insurance stored on a web-based email account, which can be accessed from any location.

Whilst, you can buy the appropriate insurance policy to protect your "people" you will still be expected to operate your event to exacting standards.

You now need to make sure you know how to comply with all the insurance conditions and then tuck the insurance policy in your back pocket.

However, it's always best to act as though you don't have any insurance cover, as this will force you to be more careful in the planning and execution of your event.

Kit

When it comes to your kit it is vital to establish who is in charge of it, and who has actual ownership. These may be different individuals or organisations. Do not make any assumptions as this can cause you problems.

If you are using the kit from the venue it may be already insured by them; or they may be expecting you to have the insurance. Either way you need to find out where you stand.

If you do need to hire equipment for your event you will usually be required to provide evidence of insurance to the kit hirer before they will allow you to take their kit away. You could also have an option to purchase their hire insurance (if they provide it).

By the way, do make sure that you know the dates that you need the kit for. Frequently the collection and delivery dates can be forgotten.

You may also need to insure the kit for the travel to and from the venue from the hire company so arrange for this to be covered. Taking care of any equipment whilst in transit is just common sense but frequently this is overlooked.

Professional packing is essential and should be a matter of routine. There is little point in arriving at your destination and discovering something has broken the equipment.

You also need to consider how you will keep kit stored securely during your event. You could be holding thousands of dollars worth of material, and professional criminal gangs have specifically targeted events for precisely that reason.

But opportunistic thieves will also be on the lookout for valuable items stored in cars, left in plain site on back seats, or even locked in boots.

When it comes to the planning, accept that things do go wrong, and knowing that you can make an insurance claim when you get back to the office won't fix your immediate problem.

So, if something did happen to an essential piece of kit, are there any local suppliers you can call on, and do you have all their contact details?

After all, the kit could be damaged in transit despite your best efforts. Or it could be that someone has forgotten that different electricity voltages operate across the globe.

Keep a track of inventory being counted in and out. If you don't know what has been delivered you will be in trouble, especially when it comes to having it returned. Event breakdowns are usually hectic periods, and people are tired, and it's all too easy for things to end up in the wrong cases, or to go "missing".

Do the people using the kit know what they are doing with it? Have they the necessary experience or are they more likely to leave you with a pile of damaged kit?

Are they familiar with how it all works or will they cause disruption through not knowing what to do?

These are some of the basics you need to address and also we recommend that you keep a paper trail to prove that you asked the right questions.

Money

While events are not always run for the purpose of making a profit, it's vital that you have a clear grasp of where the money for staging the event is coming from and when is it going to land in your bank account.

Unless you are the planner of an event where money is no object, you may need to think about the consequences of your event not happening.

Cancellation Insurance (See Insurance Section) can help protect your money from unforeseen risks.

To begin with, have a look at all the costs that you will have as you stage your event. This list could include:

- venue hire
- contractors' costs
- caterers
- marketing and promotion
- agency fees
- staff time
- banking fees
- Speaker fees

And a hundred other things, which hopefully you will have itemised on a spreadsheet.

Once you know your costs you will be able to decide how 'exposed' you could be if your event doesn't proceed.

Whilst cancellation insurance may provide some protection, it is effectively best used as a "catastrophe cover" in that it is there for all those unforeseen risks that are beyond your control.

All the normal trading risks will be down to you. If you are organising the event on behalf of a client you would be wise to point out the existence of such insurance cover.

You might also want to think about how you are going to be paid if your event, or that of a client you're working for, doesn't go ahead!

You will also need to consider the question of cash flow, monitoring how the money comes in and out. Cash flow is crucial to any business and especially so when it comes to events.

It's usual for venues, suppliers and speakers to ask for some (if not all of the payment) agreed in advance of your event opening, often before you start the marketing (which also incurs costs). And you need to get those things sorted before you can start to promote the event and generate delegate fees.

That means you need financial resources to address the initial outlay. This might come from the bank, company or personal resources. Or you may wish to underwrite some of the financial aspects by securing sponsorship; some of the money for this can then be invoiced immediately. However, do remember that, if your event doesn't go ahead the sponsors will need to be repaid.

Credit management measures will certainly help with bringing the money into your account as long as you enforce your processes well.

The basic discipline of getting your invoices paid as soon as possible can be a real benefit to you.

You will also need to decide on your refund policy if your event doesn't go ahead. Make sure you have a policy in place and ensure that everyone involved is aware of how it works if needed.

If your event is taking place outside your national borders, you may also need to factor in the issue of exchange rate fluctuations. This is a complex area but it is essential to consider the issue. After all, you might be working to a profit margin of 20%, which could be wiped out by dramatic fluctuations in currency.

Solutions to this risk do exist. You can look at agreeing the exchange rates well in advance with banks or specialist agencies, so you know exactly what the rate will be. The upside is peace of mind, and knowing that you are protected against movements that go against you.

The downside is you could lose out if the currency exchange moves in your favour. Your final decision might just be down to how "risk averse" you are as an individual or corporation.

Budgets require frequent review and adjustment. The more you know for sure about the true amount of money that is coming to you, the better it will be for you and all those involved in the event.

Do not forget about the costs and complexities of collecting money and consider any potential issues at the outset. Simple things like forgetting credit card charges or a commission payment to an intermediary such as Paypal will ultimately end up affecting the overall profitability of your event.

You also need to consider the issue of tax. You need to know or have someone who knows, what the rules are, how you comply with them, and what the various exemptions are.

You may run an event in Spain but be operating your business from France, so consider just where you pay taxes on the event, and at what rate?

Do not go out of business because you cannot pay the Taxman. Every country will have its own rules and you need to understand how they apply to you and your event.

And on the topic of money, how will you handle cash at your event? Of course, if you're organising a rock concert you'd expect large amounts of cash to be flying about, but will that apply to a business conference?

Well, you might be surprised just how much money will be used at events; it's quite common for delegates from certain countries to turn up with cash because of issues in making internet payments. So you need to have procedures in place for receiving, acknowledging, securing, banking and accounting for these situations.

It's also worth noting that staff should be briefed on how to handle the more challenging situations. For example, in Berlin in March 2010 armed robbers attacked an International Poker Tournament, stealing 242,000 Euro.

Several people were injured, mostly due to trying to escape, although fortunately no-one was seriously hurt. The basic rule to convey is that money and property, unlike people, can be replaced and should be handed over without resistance.

When it comes to the budget calculations, remember that insurance policies invariably have an "excess"(see Simple and Short Glossary of (mainly) Insurance Terms.

If you have accepted a large insurance excess to help reduce the cost of your insurance policy you will need to ensure that you have kept aside some spare funds, just in case you do need to make a claim.

Where are my Crayons?

Having carried out a major thinking exercise on the key risks of people, kit and money it is now your turn to start to evaluate the major risks to your event.

For this we recommend that you use a Top Ten Risks Ranking exercise. This need not be onerous, but the time invested up front will help you plan with confidence.

The process is relatively straightforward.

Evaluate the top ten (you can do less or more if you wish) risks to your event.

Once you have your ten risks then you need to consider how much each individual risk will critically impact on your event.

You then undertake a similar exercise to ascertain the probability of each individual risk happening.

We recommend that you use a simple scale of 1 to 10 with 1 being low and 10 being high.

In the table below we have started a fictional exercise so that you can see how this works.

Figure 4 - Example of Top Ten Risks Form

Description of Risk	Impact of Risk	Probability of Risk
Damage to the venue	7	1
Run out of cash	10	5
Speaker is ill	3	4
Food poisoning	8	2
Political instability	7	3
Impact of Legislation	5	9
New competing conference	8	6
Sufficient staffing for the conference	2	1
Kit stolen	3	8
Web streaming fails	9	4

If you plot your results on a left to right axis the Impact and from bottom to top the probability then you can view your results in a pictorial format. This will provide you with a probability vs impact grid, as shown in Figure 5.

Figure 5 - Probability vs Impact Grid

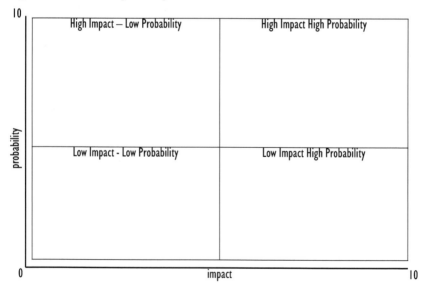

Risk It! How to Run Great Events and Live with the Risk

As far as the boxes are concerned if you have identified risks that fall within the high impact and high probability area then these will be the most immediate concerns for you to deal with in your planning.

Once you have carried out your ranking exercise you can then have a discussion amongst the key stakeholders involved in the event at which you can consider what actions you need to take.

It is also sensible to review risks on a regular basis and to factor in your thoughts and opinions on what is happening on a global scale.

Always keep looking at the wider picture. Environmental issues, identity theft, economic trends, political unrest, changing styles and demographics are just some of the factors that should be on your list to be considered.

By the way, you'll notice that neither risk nor probability ever drops to zero. That's because, as we said earlier, nothing is ever risk-free; we just learn to live with a degree of risk.

(b) More Thinking

Dealing with Risks Before they Arrive

In your earlier thinking you identified key areas that were of concern to you and the success of your event.

You looked at the connected elements of people, kit and money. From there you identified through your exercises the key risks that apply to your event.

The next stage is to work out what to do with each of the risks that you identified as being significant. As no two events are ever the same you should ensure that you are dealing with the risks that apply to your event in isolation.

For example, potential losses due to Terrorism activity may be very significant for a Defence exhibition planner in London but much less so (if at all) for a networking reception in a small town in Finland!

Whilst this may seem like a lot of work, especially if you are running a number of events, once you start the process you will be able to identify any common themes.

By carrying out this exercise on a regular basis you become more experienced and, by implication, faster at identifying and dealing with the risks.

In essence there are primarily four main ways of dealing with your risks;

> Plan B, C, D
> Insurance
> Negotiating/Contracting
> Altering/Changing the activity

Let's have a look at these in more detail.

Plans B, C, D

Have you ever noticed that "real life" can be unexpected and disruptive? Because of that, you should always consider rehearsing situations, in other words, test the plan. Factor in any new issues that come out of this part of the thinking; there will always be circumstances that we cannot foresee.

If you've ever been impressed with how quickly TV stations can produce detailed programmes when a politician or celebrity dies unexpectedly, it's because they had a programme on the shelf, frequently updated, and read to go at a moment's notice. It may sound morbid, but it pays to be prepared.

A Plan B is always a good idea, and again we can use the three elements. Here are some situations that you might like to consider.

People
What is your plan if the temporary stewards you need decide not to turn up? How will you cope?

Kit
At the last minute the vehicle delivering your staging and presentation equipment is held up in traffic. What will you do?

Money
A key sponsor decides to withdraw their sponsorship money a short time before your event is due to open. How will you handle that?

Insurance

In the "Insurance" section you will find information on policies that relate to our three elements of people, kit and money. You will discover the information that insurance companies will need to provide you with a policy.

However, some people confuse buying insurance policies with actually having really good risk plans and processes in place.

So let's be clear. Insurance will just put you back to where you were before the accident or loss happened. What it will not do is to stop or reduce any accident or injury in the first place and this is where your effective risk planning comes into its own.

If you do decide to buy insurance then make sure you understand in what situations it will actually help you.

You should also make every effort to be clear on what you need to do to ensure that your insurance policy remains valid. If you don't know what is required of you then in all probability the insurance policy will not function in the right way and you may have just wasted your money.

If you act as though you have no insurance in place you will benefit. You will benefit because you will be looking even more closely at the scenarios where things could go wrong and taking the appropriate action.

Negotiating/Contracting

For some of the risks identified you may be able to contract in a way that reduces or negates your responsibility. However, it's vital to remember that you will not be able to contract from those situations where the law of the country states that you are legally liable.

Let's look at the three areas of people, kit and money and take some examples of contracting for each:

People
Employers' Liability insurance in the UK is required by Statute. It basically means that organisations domiciled in the UK have a legal responsibility to insure their staff. So this has to be in your contracting agreements.

If you are using temporary stewards/volunteers make sure you have contracted with them so they know what is expected of them. Job descriptions can be useful here.

Kit
What are you prepared to accept as hire conditions from kit hire companies? What can you contract to your advantage?

Money
You could, as part of your contract with delegates, have "early bird" booking discounts. You might decide to have penalty clause payment terms for suppliers that do not deliver or for those people that owe you money and haven't paid by an agreed date.

How effectively you negotiate terms with a venue and or other contractors will be principle factors that affect how strong or weak your position will be.

If you have a key performer that is making unreasonable demands that you have to comply with then again this is something that you should take time to negotiate fully at the outset before the final contract is signed.

Some of the "riders' (additional terms in the contracts) can be expensive and often unrealistic and absurd, and you should be prepared for some tough negotiation rather than just accepting them without question.

Altering/Changing Your Activity

Sometimes your event planning will take on new levels of creativity which could create a whole new set of risks. It is easy to be very ambitious with events.

The key is for you and your event planning team to agree just what is and what is not acceptable.

If you decide that you really need to include hazardous activities within your event than make sure that you gather all the specialist advice on offer and take the measures needed to make the activity a success.

If you do decide that your event cannot go on without the fire-eaters you do at least have precautions in place to deal with any resulting fire.

Figure 6 - Your Risk Options

Plan B, C, D	Insurance
Negotiating/Contracting	Altering/Changing the activity

In some cases you may need to be looking at using more than one of these methods to minimise the risk to your event.

Having identified your key risks and understanding the four key ways you have to deal with them you will now be in a position to draw up your risk plan.

(c) Your Risk Plan

Making Your Risk Plan

We can now start to bring together the work you have just undertaken to start to develop your risk plan.

Figure 7 – Simple Template to Start Your Risk Plan

Risk Description	Plan B	Insurance	Negotiate	Alter
Damage to venue				
Run out of cash				
Speaker is ill				
Food poisoning				
Political instability				
Impact of legislation				
New competing conference				
Sufficient staffing for the conference				
Kit stolen				
Web streaming fails				

The risk description comes from your list of 10 that you identified in the earlier risk ranking exercise.

(As an illustration we have inserted the risks from our original fictional example. Just to demonstrate how simple the process can be).

Then you can allocate which action(s) you will take from the four methods available.

Of course you can enhance your plan, broaden it, make comments etc. The template provided is merely to help get you started.

Less is More

A detailed and lengthy risk plan that sits on a shelf ignored by everyone will be of no use.

Your plan has to be one that is easily located and updated, and its existence communicated to everyone involved. It should also be straightforward and accessible. Copies located outside the office are examples of good practice.

Your plan will ideally be free from technical jargon, but if this is used then the terms need to be defined. Anyone involved in your event should be able to pick up the plan understand what actions need to be taken.

If you are the event planner and have all the information in your head, that's of little help to your team if you become ill or are unavailable, on a long-haul flight perhaps, and they encounter a problem.

Problem Solving Mindset

When you encounter a challenge you have to find a way of overcoming it. If you run in straight lines you could go out of business very quickly.

A lateral thinking and problem-solving mindset will really help when you come up against the many challenges in organising an event.

You and your team should look at the situation in a number of different ways. Invariably there will be a suitable approach that can be used.

Eye on the Horizon

Make sure you are aware of the changing political, legal, and environmental situations that may affect your event.

We recommend that you make full use of the weather, travel and news information, all easily found by searching relevant websites.

Keeping your eye on the horizon will also ensure that you can include any new changes to your risk planning.

At this point it would be useful to keep at the very front of your mind those essential key elements of your event and establish if anything has changed that you now need to consider or add to your plan.

See our (by now) familiar People, Kit and Money Triangle.

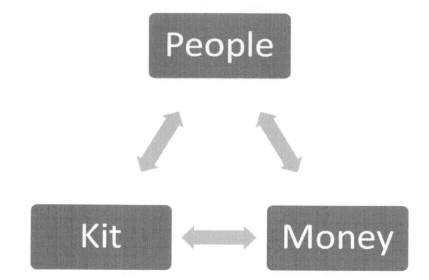

Section 3:
Action Stations

Risk It

Risk It! How to Run Great Events and Live with the Risk

Section 3:
Action Stations

Putting your Plans into Place – Crisis Occurs

In Section 1 we provided some of the risks you will need to deal with in the key elements of people, kit and money. You then decided which risks would be the most challenging for you. In Section 2 you looked at the key ways of dealing with your risks and developed a risk plan.

At this point it would be great if you could arrange a fictitious crisis scenario to test your risk plan and establish what new risks have come to light.

The test doesn't have to be a full rehearsal but could be a simple 'table top discussion' with the key stakeholders. It is always best to test what you have in your risk plan before a real crisis occurs.

The rest of this Section deals with what you need to consider regardless of whether the crisis is fictional or real. As well as your risk plan you will also need a 'communications plan' and a 'who will face the media position'. Your risk plan is one part of dealing with risks that can occur but you will also need to use other techniques at your disposal.

These include:
> Communication
> Facing the Media
> Collaboration
> Negotiation

Communication is Key

You need to have a Communications plan.

Make sure your team all understand their roles. It is also vital to ensure that mechanisms are in place to inform delegates if your event has been cancelled, postponed, or has changed in some way.

Communicating effectively is also a great way of managing expectations. Even if there is bad news to give it is best to deliver it quickly.

The worst thing you can do is to keep quiet as then you will have the "rumour mill" to deal with. If you don't give a clear explanation of the situation, others will draw their own, often wildly incorrect, conclusions.

Facing the Media

Depending on the scale of your crisis you may be in the front line of media interest. You need to be able to deal effectively with the media both in person and on line.

As well as the traditional print and TV media, do not underestimate the power of the social media outlets.

The huge growth of this sector, e.g. Facebook, Twitter, YouTube, and its ability to harness and lead public opinion must not be overlooked.

There are key skills involved in ensuring that you get your media message across professionally. This could be an area where a specialist advisor or company is bought in. One of the keys is to ensure that you have the right person talking to the media on the front line. This may not be the top person in the company. But before you get to this point you need to have decided who that person will be.

As with all audiences, media people will wait for only so long before they speculate on what is happening so ensure your media messaging is not left 'in the air' because you had not planned for having to deal with the media.

Collaboration

At a time of crisis you may find yourself working with people that were previous competitors. The key point is to be aware that it may be necessary in the short term to develop new processes or work with people that would not have previously occurred to you.

The best advice is to listen to ideas and act as you need to. In other words do not rule anything out.

Negotiate Again?

Just as with the communication and media messaging to external audiences, it's just as vital that you keep your suppliers in the loop.

At a time of crisis it is more important than ever that you keep them advised of your position on a regular basis.

The first stage is to establish what you need to do to get out of your situation, and then contact your main suppliers. You'll invariably find that word travels fast, and you'll be surprised at what they already know.

Honesty is the best policy in these situations. It may be that you need to renegotiate on fees and payment terms. If there is an issue with payment, you could discuss extending the credit period. Alternatively, you may need to get hold of more kit/finance at short notice, in which case a conversation with your bank would be sensible.

It's at times like this that having a detailed risk plan and copies of your insurance to hand will be useful negotiating tools. If suppliers and banks can see that you are protected, they may simply see your current problem as being similar to a cash-flow problem, and therefore provide to extend your credit. Without that documentation to hand suppliers might feel that providing you with more resources is like "throwing good money after bad."

Section 4:
Reflection and More Thinking

Risk It

Section 4: Reflection and More Thinking

In the last section (Action Stations) you put all those measures in place from your earlier thinking, to deal with your crisis (whether real or fictitious).

Now is the time to carry out a de-brief and work out ways in which you can learn from whatever your challenge was.

What Just Happened?

An evaluation of what happened and how you can learn from the crisis is fundamental to being in a better position for future risk planning. There needs to be a full de-brief following every situation so that everyone can learn.

Marks Out of 10

Honesty and truth are key here to learn from what happened. There is a critical time to debrief which is immediately after the event. There will be lots of information that people will still have in their heads. This needs to be written up so that you have good statements to work from.

Key questions will need to be asked in a way that encourages constructive feedback and not negativity or defensiveness. Many people are used to "blame" cultures, or may be keen to express anger at a person, department or organisation they feel has "let us down".

The questions that are asked will enable you to learn so consideration as to how they are presented needs careful thought. You should not be seeking to allocate blame but rather to be in a better position in the future.

You may also find it useful to revisit the situation a month later. Some distance from the crisis may give you and others a slightly different perspective on your thinking which again will only help you in the long run.

Back to Thinking Again

Plug all of your findings into the pre-emptive thinking. It's a continuous cycle of learning and adapting to be better prepared for the next time something crops up, which it will.

It's also worth sharing your issues with other like-minded professionals. On the following pages we have an example of how leading event education website Planet Planit (www.planetplanit.biz) asked its readers for advice when an Icelandic volcano erupted and created chaos for airlines in 2010.

Keep reviewing the event risk triangle for new challenges and you will be as prepared as you can be.

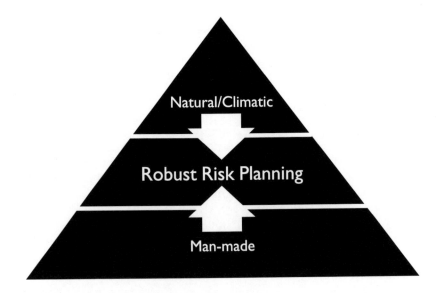

Figure 8 - Case Study: Volcanic Ash Cloud 2010

Volcanic Disruption Advice for Event Planners

by Various Event Professionals in Less than 140 Characters

At Planet Planit we used Twitter to ask some great event professionals for "The one best piece of advice to help event planners deal with the volcanic disruption issues."

These are their responses:

@mediacoach
Offer webinars from speakers to those attendees that cannot make it. Offer DVDs too. For every future event look at virtual delivery methods.

@lizkingevents
Be creative - Think of alternative travel options and creative ways to take guests minds from the disruption.

@kimgeralds
As soon as the travel advisory came out we contacted our Travel Agent to re - route our attendees before other travellers started re - booking. Best to act quick.

@miguelseven
Consider all travel options including shuttle services, rail travel and private cars.

@lyksumlikrish
Make use of the internet. Sites like Tiny chat and Stickam offer great possibilities for impromptu video conferencing.

@inspirationguy
Use social media to keep in touch. Set up micro sites if necessary to help keep your attendees informed and connected.

This response was sent by Eric Lukazewski by email. It's longer than 140 characters but as it contains such great advice, we felt it needed to be included here:

@ericlukazewski
"We had a similar crisis during 9/11, although I was not in the industry at the time. I know some major tradeshows had to be canceled because of the travel restrctions.

However, in the 8-1/2 short years since, technology and social media has proven able to facilitate certain instances where face to face isn't possible.

My advice from this would be to develop a backup plan. While large conventions and tradeshows can't quite be emulated, conferences can adapt to virtual spaces, if the proper channels are there.

A successful virtual meeting cannot be an afterthought and I believe can damage the reputation of a conference if attendees cannot interact and receive the information they need.

While situations like this are unique and many might resist a backup plan to the degree I'm suggesting, I think it can be put in to action in a number of ways if/when a large group of attendees that are crucial to your event suddenly cannot, be it weather, financial restrictions, etc. An action plan needs to come with the logistics to deliver the content, but also give proper notifications and timely understandings of how they are to use those tools." your future events.

The Lesson
When the crisis has blown over (literally in this case) that is when it is wise to consider incorporating your lateral thinking (from having developed your risk plan and then by dealing with the crisis) into your planning for your future events.

Section 5:
Insurance

Risk It!

Risk It! How to Run Great Events and Live with the Risk

Section 5: Insurance

Types of Insurance Policy

Selecting an insurance policy should be a relatively simple task. However, given the many options available and the complexity of the insurance language, the task of buying a policy can sometimes be a daunting one.

Here are some general notes on the basics of policies and how they can be found.

Key Elements
Broadly the term 'event insurance' is generic. Many policies offering 'event insurance' should be providing insurance for the following areas:

People
This is usually referred to as Liability insurance. In general terms this element of cover will provide protection to you for injury to people and damage to property (that is not yours)

Kit
Insurance companies have various names for this cover; it can be known as property/contents/kit/equipment and there may be other combinations.

Generally this insurance will cover you for damage/theft of kit that is owned/hired to you.

Money
The event insurance world refers to this as 'Cancellation' insurance. Basically the protection here is for the finances of the event. If an event is cancelled due to a reason beyond the control of the planner then this insurance is the one that is the most important.

Packages
It is possible to buy these insurances (People – Liability, Kit and Money – Cancellation) on their own. Sometimes you will not need all the elements, and buying insurance that you don't need is a waste of your money.

On occasion you may wish to buy separate elements, as it may work out cheaper or provide a better level of cover.

On the other hand, some packaged insurance policies provide great value for money and they have been devised with specific events in mind. Examples include; wedding insurance, fireworks insurance and exhibitor insurance.

When buying a packaged policy you are strongly advised to look at the various Limits of cover that will apply. If a Limit of cover is not enough for you then you may need to buy an alternative insurance.

Time Periods
In the event insurance world you can buy policies that cover just a single event, or a number of events, or you can buy an annual policy.

Single Event
This type of policy will relate to just one event. It can be useful if you organise just one event per year such as an annual dinner or a fete.

Multi Event
This will cover the number of events that you decide to insure. You could have five events per year and decide to insure them in one custom made policy.

Annual Insurance
If you have a lot of events to plan in the year on a regular basis it could be that this is the best way forward for you.

This way you can guarantee that any new events can be automatically included without you needing to keep advising your insurance company each time you add a new event (subject to the agreement you have with your insurance company).

How to Buy Insurance

Depending on where you are in the world will determine the method by which you buy an insurance policy.

In general terms there are two main ways that insurance can be bought:

- via insurance brokers/advisors

- direct from the insurance company by phone or via the internet

You may find you have no choice but have to buy via an insurance broker/advisor. If this is the case you will need to check that the insurance broker/advisor is authorised to sell insurance to you.

If there is a Regulatory body they will be responsible for making sure that the seller adheres to all the requirements (which offers you protection from any possible 'rogue operators')

If you decide and are able to buy direct via an insurance company either by phone or over the web you will benefit from the process (usually being nice and quick). However, you will need to be absolutely sure that the insurance policy will provide the cover you need.

Whatever kind of policy you decide to buy always ask the 'what if' questions, as they can be a very effective way of establishing just how well the insurance will respond if a claim occurs.

Quick Principles

Making a Proposal

As with any Contract there have to be certain key legal elements that are met for the contract to be valid. In certain parts of the world when the insurance contract becomes enforceable will differ but for ease you would be recommended to consider the following sequence.

There has to be made an offer made by you to the insurance company. Your application is the proof that you are seeking insurance.

Usually you will be required to complete a proposal form (as specified by the insurance company). This form will have a number of questions and based on your responses the insurance company will decide either to offer an insurance policy to you or not. They are under no obligation to provide insurance to you.

On the basis that the insurance company offers you a policy you can decide whether to accept or not.

If you do accept then you will be required to pay the price of the insurance (normally referred to as the insurance premium, plus any taxes/and/or administration charges/fees).

If there is no offer, acceptance or payment then the insurance contract would be voidable, i.e. in other words there would be no insurance in place.

Your completed proposal form is your statement to insurers. They will base their assessment of how much to charge, what conditions to place on your policy or whether to offer insurance in the first place.

Sometimes an insurance company will use a "Statement of Fact" which is essentially where the information you provided either on the phone or by e mail/mail is re-iterated back to you.

Sometimes you may be asked to sign the Statement but more often the receipt (by you) of the statement (from the insurance company) is all that is needed.

Disclosing All

All insurance companies will expect all 'Material' facts to be disclosed to them. Now this becomes interesting because how do you know whether a fact is material or not?

You don't want to have a problem if a loss occurs and for the insurance company to say that you didn't disclose everything. So, what should you do?

It is a tough one but if you work on common sense principles you should be fine. For example, if you are holding a conference you can be pretty sure that an insurance company will expect you to hold some training sessions, some networking events, a degree of hospitality and that would be reasonable.

Now, if you decide that you want a 'fire eater' to perform at your conference and haven't advised your insurance company, there could be a problem as many insurance companies would not expect a fire eater to be a usual fixture at a conference!

Insurance companies place a heavy emphasis on you disclosing information. But don't worry; disclosure is really nothing more than ongoing communication between you and your insurance company.

If you are in doubt, then just let the insurance company know what you are doing.

It is always better to be on the safe side and no insurance company will object to you giving them too much information.

One of the insurance principles is that of 'Utmost Good Faith' – which means that you (as the Insured) have passed all your information to insurers on all that you know. You have nothing hidden and no false statements have been made.

Just One More Thing

Insurance companies can make their own enquiries but in reality they rely on the information that you provide to them. They can check points of the information and ask for extra questions to be answered, but given the sheer volume of enquiries coming in they depend on you.

If you make a false statement or don't tell them something that they consider to be important, they can take action which may not be good for you, e.g. cancelling a policy or refusing to give insurance in the first place.

But on the basis that you have a policy and all is going well, then if you decide to embark on a new activity that your insurers don't know about, you must tell them.

It's just to be on the safe side and they can adjust your policy accordingly or make arrangements for a new one.

This disclosure requirement continues over the life of your insurance policy, so it's as well to have a good understanding of just what cover is provided.

People – (Liability) Insurance

The people cover is one of the most important elements to consider when running any event. Called simply people cover by us for ease, the insurance world will provide any number of different terms; such as Public Liability/ Third Party Liability/ General Commercial Liability/Employer's Liability to name a few.

But the essence of the cover is to protect you as the event planner from claims by a whole variety of people for injury to them. This could include claims from groups such as employees, staff, volunteers and stewards.

At the same time there will also usually be some cover included for damage to Third Party Property (i.e. property that is not yours). The most common example is that there would be cover for any damage to the venue in which you are holding your event (as long as you do not own the venue).

All Sorts of People

In Section 2 – What are they all bringing to the table - we looked at the numerous different types of people that are needed when it comes to running events.

We said that each party should only be responsible for the activity that they are carrying out and that same philosophy applies here.

You should only be insuring for your activity and you shouldn't be insuring people that you have no authority or control over.

Different Cultures and Countries

Each country will have its own particular rules and regulations that apply to insurance requirements. As the event planner you need to either understand what these are yourself or take the advice of your insurance company/broker/ advisor.

Some countries will insist on insurance policies being a compulsory requirement and you could be subject to fines/imprisonment or disqualification not to comply appropriately.

Can You Hold Your Event?

In addition to any National requirements in some districts/regions there are some venues that require evidence of insurance before they will allow you to hold your event. Sometimes it is not just venues but the local government authority. Just be sure that you understand what is required.

You may in some instances be surprised by the Limit of Liability insurance that they are asking for you to hold.

However, you also need to be happy with the Limit of cover you are buying not least because the volume and value of claim awards are forever increasing. So you need to ensure that you will have enough protection.

Basic Questions from Insurance Companies

Single event

- Number of people
- Number of employees/volunteers/stewards
- Venue/location
- Type of event
- Limit of cover required

Annual policy

- Estimated annual turnover
- Payments to sub contractors
- Estimated annual wages
- Business description
- Countries where insurance is needed
- Limit of cover required

Claims Examples

- Slips, trips and falls
- Facial injury caused by fireworks
- Damage to Third Party Property

Kit Insurance

Anything that is portable we have effectively included under the 'kit' insurance heading. This could include audio visual items, portable loos and marquees. Basically, anything that isn't a permanent structure such as a building within our definition.

For ease, the word 'kit' has been used but many insurance companies could name this type of cover other terms such as Property or All Risks, etc.

The important point is not to become confused by the language of the insurance companies in their definitions but to understand primarily where 'kit' insurance could be important to you.

Is it Mine or Yours?

Often event planners consider that kit is already insured by someone else. They might say, hand on heart, that they are not responsible. However, previously, we advised you to double check this so you can be absolutely sure.

If you do need to insure 'kit' you will need to have a good idea of the replacement cost of the kit. If you have the exact replacement costs then that is even better.

Be as close to the correct amount as possible as you don't want to insure for too little or too much.

To make the task simpler, group items under generic headings. You will find this works well for you in communicating with the insurer.

Being under-insured could leave you out of pocket if you make a claim; but being over-insured is wasting money, as the insurer will not pay you more than the items are worth.

I Don't Like Redheads or Dollies

Given the huge variety of 'kit' that insurance companies cover you can be sure that not all the insurance people that you speak to will understand everything that needs to be insured for you.

Items that are widely understood present no problem but it's when you begin to require insurance on less well known items that you will be best to describe them in more detail.

"Redheads" or "Dollies" will be widely known by people who use them in film production and any insurance company that specialises in that area will have no problem understanding what is needed. However, an insurer that is more generalist could wonder what on earth you are talking about!

The last thing you want is a situation where the insurance company don't understand what you're trying to insure, and you end up with a claim they refuse to deal with!

It sounds basic, but just make sure that your insurance company really understands what your kit is.

Hire Charges Going On and On

If you do end up hiring 'kit' have a look on your contract with the hire company for 'continuing hire charges'. These are a financial penalty that can be imposed on you for failure to return the kit on time and in a condition that it can be re-hired. If you don't return the 'kit' ready to be hired again then the hire company will lose money by not being able to hire it to their next client. And they may seek to recover their losses from you.

It's worth noting that "continuing hire charges" are not always highlighted by the hiring company, and may just be hidden away in the small print.

If you do find you are responsible for them let your insurance company know as they can usually build the financial provision for continuing hire charges cover into your policy. This will then protect your financial outlay if there is damage or loss.

We recommend that you take care to check and be clear on what could happen if the kit you hired is returned from you in a damaged state or, even worse, not returned at all.

If anything should go wrong and you need to make an insurance claim, it's important that you get the necessary independent statements, which could include a police report.

This can be quite a bureaucratic process in some countries, especially as the reports may be produced in a language with which you have no familiarity, but without these reports making a claim will prove challenging.

Basic Questions from Insurance Companies

- Is cover needed for a single event or is it needed for the year?

- Dates of cover needed – very important to include the collection and return dates (if you are hiring kit)

- Geographical Limits – where will you be using the 'kit'?

- Any previous losses/claims in the last 5 years

- Replacement cost to be insured

If you can split the replacement cost of the items between at least the following categories, insurance companies will be delighted:

- Plasma/3D screens

- Audio Visual

- Marquees/Temporary structures

- All other equipment

If you break down the 'kit' into other categories then you really will make them very happy.

Claims Examples

- Stolen laptops

- Damage to audio visual kit

- Storm damage to marquees

Money – (Cancellation Insurance)

One of the key insurance policies that you need to be aware of is the Cancellation insurance. In essence this coverage is there for the protection of your finances.

As we've seen, any event will require some money to be spent to make it happen. Contracts of all sorts have to be negotiated and agreed and then payment has to change hands. Suppliers will expect payment to be made regardless (in most cases) of whether your event goes ahead.

Cancelling Your Event is Out of Your Hands
Of course, cancelling your event is probably the last thing on your mind. However, remember the cancellation of an event is often out of your hands.

In some instances you may be able to postpone your event. Moreover, cancellation insurance is also in force once the event has started and then has to be abandoned or curtailed. All of these scenarios are covered by a Cancellation insurance policy.

Whilst you are not looking for your event to be anything other than an amazing success it is the unknown risks that can come along and bring you a whole new set of challenges to deal with.

A quick look over recent years will remind us of the disruption and chaos caused by SARS, Foot and Mouth Disease, Avian Flu, Terrorism incidents, and the volcanic ash cloud.

These are the most high-profile examples, but many event planners have claimed from their cancellation insurance for a host of other reasons.

Even with a wealth of history at the disposal of insurance companies it is impossible to determine all the scenarios that could lead to your event to be cancelled due to some reason beyond your control.

Because of this (most) Cancellation insurance policies provide an all-encompassing range of cover. However, there will be Exclusions and it is these that you have to make time to fully understand.

This is different to those policies that state that a certain situation has to occur for cover to operate.

If you don't understand the Exclusions and what they mean then ask your insurance company/advisor/broker for a thorough explanation.

It is important that you understand about the availability of this product even if you decide not to buy the insurance. The same applies when you are acting for clients or sponsors.

If you understand the product (at least in broad terms) you, and your clients will be able to understand any financial exposure if the event is cancelled.

You can decide to insure just your costs of holding your event but in some cases you can also insure your profit element.

Profit can usually be insured on the basis of pre-sold tickets or using calculations based on an audited three year history of ticket sales that can be supplied to the insurance company.

Not Just the Deposit

Often event planners have been known to say that it is just the deposit (paid to the venue) that is their risk exposure.

However, this is usually not the case. The Contract (between you and the venue) will state the financial amount that will need to be paid, regardless of whether your event goes ahead, and this will be indicated on the contract (although if you are a skilled negotiator these terms can be amended to work more in your favour).

So to protect your financial position as effectively as possible the time to buy Cancellation insurance (if you decide to) is as soon as you sign the contract with the venue or any other supplier.

The good news is that many insurance companies allow for events to be insured usually eighteen months or more from the moment at which you ask for the insurance to start.

Financial Guarantee

One of the key questions that a lot of event planners have is whether a Cancellation policy will pay out if not enough tickets are sold. The answer is "no"; because insurance companies view the lack of sales as being down to you as the Planner. A Cancellation insurance policy is not a financial guarantee insurance.

Basic Questions from Insurance Companies

- Venue address (es)/Location
- Date(s) of the event
- Type of event – full description of activities always helps
- Monetary amount to be insured
- Is there a dependency on a key speaker/performer that could lead to cancellation (see Non Appearance)
- Is there a dependency on the weather (see Bad Weather)•

Claims Examples

A whole host of simple errors can cause an event to be cancelled, postponed, abandoned or curtailed. Some common scenarios are outlined:

- Denial of access to the venue where your event is due to be held
- Disruption of electricity, gas, or water following a worker cutting a cable by mistake or similar
- Damage to the venue
- Unexpected strike action

Money – (Cancellation) Non Appearance Insurance

Cancellation insurance can be extended to include Non appearance cover. This insurance protection is very useful if your event is dependent on a key speaker or performer turning up.

Key Speaker is Stuck

It could be a key speaker, or it could be an act to entertain your Dinner guests. If this person/act isn't able to make it what will be the impact on your event?

How much money will you have lost, if you have to provide refunds? Will you have to give all, or just a percentage back? Will it come from your reserves, will it come from your client (if you are an agent) or could it be that the sponsors demand their money back?

As you will have gathered by now the reason for your key speaker or performer not being able to turn up has to be beyond their control.

When the 9 /11 Terrorist attacks took place a number of speakers were unable to complete their flights to the United States from the UK and ended up being diverted to Canada.

Clearly this was a situation beyond their control.

Fortunately insurance companies offer non-appearance insurance primarily for accident or illness of the performer/speaker/act.

However, some acts may not be able to be insured especially if there is a history of no shows for their performances.

Basic Questions from Insurance Companies

- Age of the person
- Where travelling from
- Schedule of activity of the person prior to your event
- Health of the person
- Any previous claims
- Monetary amount to be insured

Claims Examples

Again there can be any number of reasons for your key speaker/performer not being able to take to the stage. Here are some common illustrations:

- Accident
- Illness
- Flight cancellation/diversion

Money – (Cancellation) Bad Weather Insurance

Cancellation insurance can be extended to include bad weather cover. This insurance protection is very useful if your event is dependent on the weather.

The key issue for you to decide is whether the weather is an issue for you. Outdoor events in some countries may be very susceptible to the weather, although many outdoor events will continue regardless of the weather.

If you decide to buy this cover then you will need to do so at least 14 days in advance of the event date.

The reason? Less than 14 days and it's probable that you could anticipate the likely conditions from the weather forecasts.

Is the bad weather insurance really essential to you? Would you really not be able to carry on? If you carry on because you are concerned about financial losses it has to be with safety in mind as your legal and reputational position could be comprised if you make a poor decision.

Didn't See That Typhoon Coming

If you decide that you need the insurance be sure to understand the seasons and local variances that will impact your event. For example, trying to obtain bad weather cover in a known hurricane season is unlikely to be successful. This may sound obvious but some event planners juggling a variety of events in a pressurized work environment could miss this.

Insurance companies can offer Bad Weather insurance. You will need to be clear when you want the insurance cover to start from, so do allow for set-up dates to be included.

It is not worth starting the insurance cover from the first day of the event if you need extra days insured for set-up. A typical scenario could be to lay down security fencing prior to the event opening.

Basic Questions from Insurance Companies

- Venue/Location – especially proximity to rivers
- Period of cover needed – is it 1 day or several days
- Any previous claims due to flooding, waterlogging etc
- Monetary amount to be insured

Claims Examples

The weather is such a factor in the success of many outdoor events that it is always worth paying respect to. Here are some typical examples where the weather made its presence known:

- Festivals rained off
- Strong winds forcing events to close
- Frost causing horse racing meetings to be cancelled

Terrorism Insurance (Protecting Money)

Over recent years some event planners have determined that Terrorism Insurance is essential for their own peace of mind and also that of their sponsors/clients.

Scary to Consider Explosions

Unfortunately often in the news, we live in times when terrorist attacks can occur virtually anywhere and at almost any time.

The availability of Terrorism Insurance changes according to the times. But the real issue for you is to decide whether you believe that your event or exhibition could be affected by terrorists. This is a specialist area and terms and pricing available from insurers change frequently.

Some insurance policies may have certain levels of cover already provided as standard. But there will be restrictions on the extent and also the circumstances in which the Terrorism cover would be triggered.

For example, some polices will provide insurance up to an agreed monetary limit on the basis that the event occurs within so many miles of the venue holding the event and within a certain time period from the start date of the event. So the cover may be nice to have but you need to be aware of its limitations. (The limitations will vary between insurance companies.)

The lack or prevalence of Terrorism activity directly affects the pricing that insurance companies charge for cover.

Insurance companies will need to know where your event is going to be held. Some countries are more prone than others to Terrorism attacks.

Types of Cover

Time and Distance
Terrorism event takes place and is covered if within a certain date and time according to the insurance company policy.

Host Country
Terrorism is covered without time and distance restrictions within the country where the event is due to be held.

Cross Border
This is the wider form of Terrorism insurance so that you are covered if your event is affected by a Terrorist event that takes place in a country that is not the host country of your event.

Short term policies are available as well as annual cover. Your choice will be for which level of cover and for what time period.

Basic Questions from Insurance Companies

- Where will the event be held, country and venue?
- What is the amount of money/Limit to be Insured?

Claims Examples

- Many examples occur on a regular basis and some have been highlighted already in Section 1 – Events and Risks.

Travel Insurance

Travel Insurance is another insurance product that you may wish to consider.

As the event planner you may have your own insurance in place simply due to the number of site visits you are required to carry out. Even if you are a domestic event planner it could still be worth considering.

Travel Insurance policies will include all sorts of different elements of cover (e.g. baggage, money, cancellation) but the key to look for is the medical repatriation expenses. This is the cover that will ensure that you or your party can be air lifted to safety or ferried to hospital.

Don't I Have this Cover Somewhere?
You may want to check what Travel Insurance you already have. You may already have a policy in place; some insurance companies provide a degree of cover under a Household policy but it is unlikely that this is sufficient for your purposes.

The same consideration applies to some of the credit cards that offer travel insurance. You would really need to check whether they have any business insurance that you could use. So just be careful.

If you do have the cover then you will not need to buy it again. However, if you decide that you need to provide some travel insurance for your delegates then you would be well to speak to your insurance company/adviser.

Again the different Regulatory bodies that oversee insurance selling in certain countries could have an impact on what you can or cannot buy in your capacity as the event planner. This is subject to change so be sure to always seek the latest advice.

Pay Less Pay More: You Decide
You can buy this insurance on-line, you can buy when you are sitting with your travel agent and of course you can buy via an approved and regulated insurance intermediary.

There are a huge number of different travel insurance policies on the market, and prices vary but as with most products if you pay cheap you may pay twice. The market is huge and there a great number of insurance companies offering cover.

Some people decide to buy on line and take the very cheapest option. Others will pay more and may buy insurance through an insurance broker/advisor. As always the choice is yours.

The price that you pay will depend on a number of factors, such as; where you are going, for how long, for what purpose, and what levels of cover you need.

Basic Questions from Insurance Companies

- How many trips will you be making this year?
- What is the length of your trip?
- What will you be doing whilst on your trip?

Sometimes a single trip policy may be best, but as a rule of thumb if you undertake more than two/three it could be advisable to look at an annual policy.

Where will you be going? This may seem an obvious question but be sure that you pay the right price for the right area. You should also check that the country is not excluded by the insurance company; some countries are definite "no go" areas.

Checking the websites of the various on line Government agencies will help here. Most will have up to date information on "hot spot" countries and many have tips to make your trip more enjoyable.

However, do be aware that some of these official websites do sometimes play on the negative aspects of a country, so always make sure your delegates understand the actual position.

Key Questions You Need to Ask

What are the Exclusions?
This is a key question in general and also if you like skiing or diving, as policies may have limitations. You may need to pay extra for skiing and you will need to be aware of the diving depth allowed.

Am I covered for loss due to Terrorism?
Some policies will include this in exchange for an additional premium being paid.

What are the Medical Expenses and Repatriation Limits?
This is a critical area as far as we are concerned. There is little point in having great baggage cover if you cannot be air-lifted to safety.

Claims Examples

Here is a sprinkling of typical claim scenarios that travel insurers deal with on a regular basis:

- Death of a close relative leading to cancellation of the trip
- Loss of baggage
- Injury/illness of person due to travel

First Aid Kit

First Aid kits and insurance policies really perform the same basic function. They both provide some degree of comfort at a time of injury or loss.

The First Aid kit can help stop the bleeding and the insurance policy can help to put you back on the road to recovery with your business. Both perform at times of crisis but neither is a substitute for making sure that you have taken as much care to protect yourself or your organisation.

In other words having an insurance policy will never take away the need for you to exercise controls to keep your event as free as you can from harm or loss.

Where Has it Gone?

A First Aid kit should always be stocked up and ready to be used. No doubt you will have tucked away your First Aid kit somewhere where you can easily find it.

The same principle applies for your insurance papers or you could be in trouble. There will be little point in having insurance if at the critical point you are unable to find the papers.

One simple tip would be to have the policy numbers, description of the cover and contact information kept on a separate sheet of paper that you keep in a safe place. That way, if you have mislaid the bundles of papers that insurance companies and brokers send to you at least you will have enough information (from your single sheet) to begin a conversation.

Ready for Use

As with a First Aid kit you will need to know where your insurance papers are so they can be found checked and updated. It is the same with your First Aid kit as replacing plasters/bandages for those that have been used. Having a field bandage in your First Aid kit is no use if you don't know how to apply it.

Similarly, having an insurance policy is no use to you if you do not understand how the cover operates and what conditions you have to comply with.

So check that you know what is required of you, otherwise the insurance policy is just a piece of paper that will not help.

Take on Your Next Trip

If you don't use your First Aid kit on a trip you wouldn't leave it behind the next time. You would still take it. The same thinking applies here to your insurance policies.

Just because you may not have needed to make a claim this time it doesn't mean that you won't need to in the future.

In times of a poor economic situation some event planners have chosen not to buy insurance in exchange for a short term cost saving.

It could be a risky plan and it could work but you will not lessen the risk of needing insurance by not taking any.

Section 6:
Sector Challenges

Risk It

Section 6:
Sector Challenges

The model we've used so far has been based on that of an event planner delivering a single event.

This provides an ideal start point to develop risk thinking for many events and other situations.

So now let's add a few specifics under the following headings that may be useful. You may find them worth reading, regardless of where you work.

Venues

Without a venue your event isn't going to get very far. Venues are so important that we believe that event professionals everywhere should be aware of their key risks.

These can include:

- Damage to the venue or fixtures/items within the venue

- Non- payment of the contracted agreed amount

- Cancellation of an event by a planner at very short notice

- Food not being delivered on time in the quantity and of the quality required

- Power disruption to the venue

- Denial of access to the venue

- Last minute change requests from the event planner which were previously not mentioned

- Inability to obtain decisions from event planners

- Ability to turn rooms around to keep to the programme schedule

- Shortage/sickness of staff

- Changes to Legislation

- Environmental pressure/requirements

It is always worth sitting down with the chosen venue and going through the contract line by line. It may not be the most fun part of event organising, but it is one of the most important. Working together will benefit you both.

Speakers

As with a venue, speakers are integral to many events although sometimes they seem to be treated by some event planners as an extra add on that is really not that valued.

Without question every speaker (especially professionals, who do it for a living) will always wish to deliver the very best they can for the event (as with all businesses they want to be referred on and invited back again). This, of course, leads to their reputation being developed and their speaker fees producing good income.

Most speakers who are confirmed will move heaven and earth to be speaking at your event. Of course, there are those unforeseen circumstances that can effect this.

The main risks to a speaker include:

- Sickness

- Accident

- Injury

- Loss of voice

- Death of a close family member/business partner

- Travel disruption or delay

- Non-receipt of speaking fee in advance of the event

- Insufficient briefing by the event organiser of any changes to the speaking engagement

- No contact with the end client (contact helps to ensure the audience receive what they came for)

- Last minute confirmation of speaking engagements (good speakers have very full diaries)

- No time for sound and stage checks

- Inappropriate content during the presentation

If you book a speaker through a bureau, then they will normally ensure that they can provide a replacement of similar calibre. However, if your audience is expecting to hear from, say, former UK Prime Minister Tony Blair, there are unlikely to be many acceptable substitutes.

If you are dealing directly with the speaker's own company, then you may want to ask questions about "what if you can't turn up?"

If your speaker doesn't show up, you should be able to recover the fees, but that may be scant comfort if you then have to cancel your event.

The same situation may also apply if you are using a non-professional speaker, for example, a senior manager from another company. If they suddenly decide to cancel, you've no way of funding a replacement at their expense (after all, you're not paying them a fee, and an official contract is unlikely to exist.

Those situations shouldn't result in your event being postponed (and you'll invariably publicise the fact that the speaker programme can change without notice) but it's one more issue that you need to be aware of.

Agency Event Planners

Many corporate companies and organisations may decide that the planning of their event is better placed by an agency event planner.

The agency event planner will work with a client or a number of clients. For an agency event planner to be successful they will have to be sure of delivering one successful event after another to make sure that their client doesn't decide to take the work in-house. (Of course, sometimes this cannot be avoided, especially in times of an economic downturn) .

The agency event planner may work across different industries and countries and different types of event so they really do need a wealth of knowledge to be effective.

Let's look at some key considerations for the agency event planner:

- Real knowledge of the client and objective(s) of their event(s)

- Broad network of contacts to easily find suppliers

- Ability to multi-task events for different clients

- Understanding of the issues that face corporate and association event planners (as the corporate or the association could be the agency's client)

As you can see the event agency planner needs to know as much as the client about the client's business to deliver successful events and to be asked back again.

This is one of the reasons some event agency planners focus on specific industry types rather than becoming a general event planner who would take on any client.

Association Event Planners

For associations (of which there are many thousands across the globe) business events can be an important part of their raison d'etre and also a valuable part of their income.

Association events can range from exhibitions to seminars, workshops to international conventions, lectures to sponsored awards dinners. All of these have certain requirements that need to be considered.

Interestingly, it's the association meetings market that has proved to be the most resilient to recent economic downturns. There are a variety of issues at play here, but one important factor is that attendance at such events can be important to obtain Continuing Professional Development (CPD) accreditation/Continuing Education Units.

That means that associations also need to consider anything that could hinder delegates who are attending specifically for this reason.

Many associations delegate the operation of these events to management companies or agencies. However, delegating the management does not mean abrogating the responsibility for effective risk planning and adequate insurance.

It's also worth remembering that the responsibility for these areas usually sits with a Board, who are often appointed for 1-3 years, so it's vital to ensure that the induction for new members includes the relevant training and explanation of the consequences.

Ultimately the Board of the Association will be responsible for anything that goes wrong. They are there to serve the 'members of the association' who are often changing as new members join and old members leave.

Here are some questions for association event planners that we think have to be considered on a regular basis:

- Is there innovation in our programme of events from last year?

- Are we using the same speakers (as they are friends)?

- Is the education content meeting the needs of our members?

- Are our events in accordance with the strategic plan of our Association?

- Are we managing expectations of "members"

- How is our association different to other associations through our programme of events?

- What is our access and availability of event sponsors?

- Do we have enough volunteers to help with the physical execution of the event(s)?

- Are we on budget and is the cash flow working?

- Are we making it easy for our members to register?

- Have we allowed sufficient time to market our event(s)?

Again, we're keen to give you a sample of just some of the more specific issues that an association event planner has to consider.

Corporate Event Planners

Some of our readers will be responsible for their company's events, and often this is just one of many areas of responsibility.

It could be far too easy to neglect the issue of risk planning and insurance, and hope that it is all taken care of by someone else or by another department.

So let us have a look at some key considerations and questions for the corporate event planner:

- Media attention

- Public perception

- Compliance with legislation

- Role of the procurement officer (department)

- Interaction between the event planner and procurement

- Adequacy of business insurance – does it extend for events?

- Payment terms with suppliers versus our in-house terms

- Communication with staff if the event cannot be held – How will we get the message across to our staff before they start on their journeys to the event?

- In the event of an emergency/crisis can we locate all our staff who were due to attend the event(s)?

- Potential of sexual harassment situations at events especially the famous Christmas party

This is just a taste but it provides an idea of some additional areas that a corporate event planner has to consider.

Help in addressing some of these risks is likely to be available from colleagues in departments such as "PR, "Corporate Communications", and "Logistics".

Festival and Outdoor Event Planners

Planners of these kinds of events have a whole new dimension to consider. There is a host of legal and operational issues that need to be considered and working through them in detail would require another book.

However here are some areas for consideration that have caught our eye:

- Accessibility for parking

- Parking on hard or soft ground

- Easy to read road signage and directions

- Road wardens/control

- Training of volunteer stewards

- First Aid provision

- Food & drink legal compliance

- Security of the site (as the build and break down of the event may span many days)

- Help point for people/children who become lost

- Evacuation procedures

- Bad weather – Plan B considerations

- Damage to underground services (be very careful)

- Accidental Pollution of the land

- Noise levels

- Consideration of neighbours/local residents

- Strong communication with emergency services

Again, this is just a taste but it provides an idea of some additional areas that a festival/outdoor event planner has to consider.

Organising such an event would require approval from local or regional authorities, the Police and a plethora of licensing agents.

Your local authority/state/district/council's website is often a good place to start for extra advice and guidance.

Summary
and a look to the future

Risk It

Risk It! How to Run Great Events and Live with the Risk

Summary
and a look to the future

In this book we have taken you on a journey and in doing so have covered a number of practical areas.

We began by advising you not to be afraid of risk but to view it as invigorating as risk keeps pushing the boundaries of change for our society. To believe that you can eliminate risks from your event in our opinion is just silly. Risk is always around us and is not going anywhere soon but there are techniques you can apply to minimise the effect of risk.

We looked at the different types of event and then commented on some of the high profile losses that have been in the media over the last few years.

But all of this was not to worry you but to bring to the table some of the very real consequences of poor risk planning.

To take the worry from you we moved on to look at how you can view your event through the key elements of people, kit and money. This was simply to stir the pot and bring out all those issues that could go wrong to help raise your awareness levels (in case they needed elevating).

We then asked you to carry out some basic risk planning techniques before providing some guidance on what to do if a crisis strikes.

From there we devoted some time investigating the event insurance world and stressed again that insurance is not an alternative to risk planning but that it is one of the techniques that can be used in your planning.

Being that risk is all around us we then investigated what risk means to some key sectors in the industry, so we looked at risks for venues, speakers, agency, association, corporate, festival and outdoor event planners. We did this on the basis that sometimes it makes sense to develop stronger business relationships by knowing what it feels like to be the other party.

This brings us then to the end. Well almost but never. You see as we have said earlier risk is going nowhere soon so we must always be looking at the future.

What does the future look like for those in the events industry?

We mentioned it earlier but event professionals will need to be aware of the changing political, legal, and environmental situations that may affect events. Then there are all the risks that we have mentioned already plus new ones.

We will just leave you with one extra example to think about:

If a performer or speaker doesn't deliver to the perceived satisfaction of a percentage of your audience or stakeholders, what happens then?

Well at this stage, frankly nothing; but could that change? If you go to a concert and feel that the artist didn't perform could you recover your money?

Our view is that litigation and public perception will continue to force new risks on our industry. Some may be justified and some not but the wise event professional will weave the new risks into their risk planning.

We recommend that you make full use of the weather, travel and news information, all easily found by searching relevant websites.

Keeping your eye on the horizon will also ensure that you can include any new changes to your risk planning.

Good luck, the future is bright. Risky as ever, but bright!

Glossary
Links
Resources

Risk It

Risk It! How to Run Great Events and Live with the Risk

Glossary
a simple & short glossary of (mainly) insurance terms

The aim of this glossary is to provide you with the explanation of some key words/phrases that we have used in Risk It! In some instances we have changed the strict (literal/academic) meaning of the word(s) to suit the flow of Risk It!

(And to take the jargon away from you - as far as possible!)

Quick Basics

Continuing Hire Charges
Financial penalty charges payable by the event planner if the kit returned to the equipment hire provider is not able to be used/hired out.

Contractor
A company or individual that has been contracted to carry out some role in the event. Typically, Audio Visual companies or Security fall into this category.

Event Planner
Anyone who has the role of organising an event. This definition includes agency event planners, corporate event planners, association planners, people who work in HR, or as PAs, or in similar roles and have the task of organising.

Hire Company
The company that is hiring equipment to event planners. Hire companies

could include those that hire, audio visual, portaloos, marquees, badging systems and so on..

Replacement Cost
Simply put the cost(s) of replacing an item(s). This is different to the cost the item may have been bought for. How much would be needed today to replace the item(s).

Sponsor
The organisation/individual that has provided money or funding for the event.

Some Key Terms found in Insurance Documentation

Certificate of Insurance
A document explaining the insurance cover purchased by the insured. A Certificate of Insurance does not detail all the terms, which are contained in a separate insurance policy.

Excess
The agreed amount of the losse(s)arising under an insurance contract that must be borne by the insured.

Exclusion
Excludes the insurance company from liability for specified types of loss. An exclusion may apply throughout a policy or it may be limited to specific sections of it.

Insurance
A contract whereby an insurance company promises to pay the insured after an uncertain event(s) in exchange for the payment of a premium payment by the insured.

Insurance Policy
A legal contract, which states the terms of the agreement between the insured party and the insurance company. This document will contain exclusions of warranties and other clauses, which may require to be interpreted by professionals.

Limit of Liability
This will be the total amount of the insurance that the insurance company will pay up to. It is a definite sum.

Loss
Injury,harm,damage or financial detriment that a person/organisation sustains. Losses may be insured or uninsured. Whether a loss is covered by a policy or certificate of insurance depends on the terms of that document and the local law.

Material Fact
Any fact that the insurance company needs to know to help them make their assessment of the insurance. Previous accidents/claims would be examples of a material fact.

Premium
The price charged by an insurance company in order to grant insurance cover.

Proposal (form)
This is the form that is used by insurance companies as the basis of the insurance contract. Questions are asked on the form which the proposer has to answer. The answers determine the offer or not of an insurance policy.

Sum Insured
The maximum amount that an insurance company will pay under a contract of insurance.

Underwrite
The acceptance of the obligation by the insurance company to pay or indemnify the insured under a contract of insurance.

Void Policy
A contract that has no legal effect and is therefore unenforceable in a court of law.

People Involved

Insurance Company
The company who has undertaken to cover the risk of the policyholder, so that, in the event of any loss as stated in the contract, the insured party is recompensed for their loss.

Policyholder
The person who is insured under a contract of insurance.

Insurance Broker
The person or organisation who arranges insurance with an insurance company(ies) on behalf of a client

Claimant
An insured party who has undergone a loss(es), which they believe to entitle them for compensation under the terms of their insurance policy.

Insured
A person who is insured under a contract of insurance. This person is also referred to as the policyholder.

Third Party
Someone other than the insured or his insurance company..

Regulatory Body
The body that approves and regulates the selling of insurance. In the UK the body is currently the Financial Services Authority. Different countries have different Regulators.

Key Elements of Event Insurance

Cancellation Insurance
This covers the financial loss, if the event has to be cancelled, abandoned, postponed or relocated due to circumstances beyond the control of the event planner.

Kit
Our definition of kit could be described by some as Property/contents/equipment.

Liability Insurance (sometime known as Public/Third Party/General Commercial)
An insurance which covers the insured against third party claims.

Package Insurance
This is a policy that has different elements of cover included.

Useful Links and Resources

There are lots of resources available, and more are added all the time, so maintaining a complete list can be challenging. Additionally, phone numbers and addresses change, so we've worked on the basis that a web address is more likely to be effective in helping you track down and check out what support is available.

The list below could go on and on but here we have highlighted some key groups for you.

Where You Can Find Fellow Event Professionals

Association of British Professional Conference Organisers
www.abpco.org

International Association of Professional Congress Organisers
www.iapco.org

ICCA
www.iccaworld.com

Meetings Industry Association
www.meetings.org

MPI (Global)
www.mpiweb.org

MPI UK & Ireland
www.mpiuk.org

Society of Incentive Travel Executives
www.site-intl.org

National Societies of Association Executives
www.esae.org

American Society of Association Executives
http://www.asaecenter.org/

Association of Exhibition Organisers
www.aeo.org.uk

International Society of Special Events
www.ises.org

Institute of Travel and Meetings
www.itm.org.uk

Eventia
www.eventia.org.uk

Professional Speaking Association (UK)
www.professionalspeaking.biz

Global Speakers Federation
www.globalspeakers.net

Green Meeting Industry Council
www.greenmeetings.info

Business Travel Club
www.businesstravelclub.com

Great Resources for Finding People & News

Google
www.google.com

Twitter
www.twitter.com

Linked in
www.linkedin.com

Facebook
www.facebook.com

You Tube
www.youtube.com

Google Alerts
www.google.com/alerts

Experts in their Fields (that we recommend)

Alan Stevens – Media Coach
www.mediacoach.com

Ruud W Janssen – Collaboration and Technology expert
www.tnoc.ch

Samuel J Smith – Events Technology expert
www.interactivemeetingtechnology.com

Kursha Woodgate – Mexia Communications – PR expert in events
www.mexiacommunications.com

Clarity Event Insurance – Paul Cook – Event & Media Insurance Expert
www.clarityeventinsurance.com

Richard John – Events industry writer, trainer, consultant & presenter
www.rjagb.com

Create Your Own

The list of useful links and resources is almost endless but we recommend that you also consider these organisations:

Insurance Regulators
Travel Advisory organisations
Foreign Embassies
Destination Management Companies
Health & Safety Regulators
Law of the Country
Revenue & Customs Regulators
Not for Profit Guidelines
Tradeshow Publications

We are sure you can think of even more sources of information.

Another Good Idea

Why not use this sheet as a guide and update for your own benefit when you find the 'people' that you need to know. You will find a copy of this "Useful Links and Resources" sheet within the Risk Management section of the Event IQ Magazine in **www.planetplanit.biz**.

You can also subscribe to the free but valuable "Oracle" which is the e-newsletter from Planet Planit for event planners. It is issued on a regular basis (every few weeks), but don't worry your contact information will not be passed to any other organisation.

A Key Resource

Planet Planit – Raising the level of Professionalism in events
www.planetplanit.biz

References of Incidents and Legislation

These references have been compiled in the order in which they appear in the book.

Haiti Eathquake 2010
http://news.bbc.co.uk/1/hi/8455629.stm

Icelandic Volcano 2010
http://news.bbc.co.uk/1/hi/uk/8621407.stm

Tennessee Floods 2010
http://articles.cnn.com/2010-05-02/us/nashville.flooding_1_flooding-three-temporary-shelters-nashville-schools?_s=PM:US

Katowice Trade Hall roof collapse
http://news.bbc.co.uk/1/hi/world/europe/4659872.stm

Love Parade 2010
http://winnipeg.ctv.ca/servlet/an/local/CTVNews/20100724/german-love-parade-100724/20100724/?hub=WinnipegHome

Huntingdon Life Sciences
http://www.bbc.co.uk/news/uk-england-11600398

Gulf of Mexico Oil Spill
http://www.washingtonpost.com/wp-dyn/content/article/2010/04/26/AR2010042604308.html

Disability Discrimination Act 1995 (UK)
http://www.hm-treasury.gov.uk/disability_discrimination_act_1995_explained.htm

Americans with Disabilities Act of 1990
http://www.access-board.gov/about/laws/ada.htm

Bavaria Brewery (Netherlands)- Ambush Marketing
http://news.bbc.co.uk/1/hi/8743881.stm

The Yes Men
http://theyesmen.org

OECD Anti-Bribery Convention
http://www.oecd.org/dataoecd/4/18/38028044.pdf

European Poker Tour (Theft)
http://www.rounderspalace.com/ept-berlin-robbery-boss-behind-bars/

United Kingdom Labour Law
http://www.direct.gov.uk/en/Employment/Employees/index.htm

About the
Authors

Risk It

Risk It! How to Run Great Events and Live with the Risk

Paul Cook

Paul Cook has created and developed businesses specifically for the events industry.

Planet Planit Ltd is his internet publishing business. It has quickly become the website for event planners everywhere to go to for event planning information.

Clarity Event Insurance is his specialist event and media insurance brokerage.

Paul originally started his career by working in insurance. He gained his insurance qualifications and worked his way around the UK to develop his understanding of different insurance products and risk planning techniques.

He spent some time working at Pinewood Film Studios where he gained much experience of the fast-moving productions and events industries. Later he created his own insurance agency – Clarity Event Insurance.

He is a frequent guest lecturer at Universities in the UK and Europe. Paul writes on a regular basis for on-line and trade publications.

Paul's passion is connecting people and ideas. Through his businesses and his leadership in Meeting Professionals International (MPI) he is a recognised industry figure known for his pragmatic, creative and common-sense business approach.

Many people know Paul as the "Events Connector".

You can contact Paul at **paul@planetplanit.biz**

Richard John

Richard John is Managing Director of RJA (GB) Ltd, based in the UK. Richard has nearly 25 years of sales, marketing, and management experience, working with a host of international organisations.

Richard is recognised as a leading authority in the field of event management, training and consultancy. In 1996 he was appointed as a Course Director for the Teaching Faculty at the prestigious Chartered Institute of Marketing, where he lectures on all aspects of exhibition and event strategy and marketing. In 2010 he was appointed part-time Workforce Development Fellow for the University of Derby, developing new and innovative approaches to learning, training and accreditation.

Richard has a Joint Honours Degree (Economics & International Studies) from Warwick University and is completing his MSc in Conference Management at Leeds Metropolitan University. He is a Fellow of the Chartered Institute of Marketing, the Institute of Sales and Marketing Management and the Institute of Training and Occupational Learning.

He is a guest Lecturer on the Events Management programmes at Leeds Metropolitan University and University of Derby, a visiting Lecturer at Cologne University and EWS in Dresden and visiting Lecturer at the London University of the Arts. His articles on all aspects of face to face communication have appeared in more than 50 magazines and he is a regular columnist in a number of MICE magazines.

You can contact Richard at **contact@rjagb.com**